Introduction to Bookkeeping and Accounting

in a week

Roger Mason

Headway · Hodder & Stoughton

British Library Cataloguing in Publication Data

A catalogue record for this title is available from the British Library

ISBN 0 340 62742 5

First published 1995
Impression number   10   9   8   7   6   5   4   3   2   1
Year   1999   1998   1997   1996   1995

Typeset by Multiplex Techniques Ltd, St Mary Cray, Kent.
Printed in Great Britain for Hodder & Stoughton
Educational, a division of Hodder Headline Plc,
338 Euston Road, London NW1 3BH by St Edmundsbury
Press, Bury St Edmunds.

**the Institute
of Management**

F O U N D A T I O N

The Institute of Management (IM) is at the forefront of
management development and best management
practice. The Institute embraces all levels of
management from students to chief executives. It
provides a unique portfolio of services for all
managers, enabling them to develop skills and achieve
management excellence.

For information on the benefits of membership, please
write to:

Department HS
Institute of Management
Cottingham Road
Corby
Northants NN17 1TT
Tel. 01536 204222
Fax. 01536 201651

This series is commissioned by the Institute of
Management Foundation.

C O N T E N T S

■ I N T R O D U C T I O N ■

Millions of sets of accounting records are maintained. They range from the accounts of major companies, through to the cash book of such bodies as a local stamp collector's club.

An understanding of the basic principles of bookkeeping and accounts is of great importance. It will help all managers, not just those involved in keeping accounting records. With this basic understanding they will be able to deal effectively with such questions as:

- Sales are up! how can there possibly be an overdraft?
- Why does every bookkeeping entry have two sides?
- What is the accountant talking about?
- Just what *is* a contingency account?

This book is written for managers wishing to master these principles. By setting aside a little time each day for a week, you should develop the necessary understanding.

Please note that your learning on Saturday will be more effective if you have to hand a company's Annual Report and Accounts. It would be helpful if this could be obtained in advance.

The basic principles of bookkeeping

Millions of sets of accounting records are kept. At one extreme, scores of qualified accountants toil to prepare the published accounts of a major company. At the other extreme, the treasurer of a local tennis club reports on the finances to the members.

All the records, from the mightiest to the most humble should be kept according to the basic principles of bookkeeping. These are timeless and the same for all organisations. A study of basic principles is an excellent way of starting the week.

- Single entry bookkeeping
- The concept of double entry bookkeeping
- The basic rules and disciplines of double entry bookkeeping

Single entry bookkeeping

As the name suggests, single entry bookkeeping involves writing down each transaction just once. It is in fact the simple listing of income and expenditure. Numerous small organisations keep their records in this way, among them probably the tennis club mentioned earlier.

Every time the treasurer writes a cheque, he records in a book the date, amount and payee. Every time something is paid into the bank the details are entered elsewhere in the book. Cash paid out or received is entered in a similar way.

If the treasurer has been very careful he can prepare an accurate receipts and payments account from the records. He would, however, be wise to prove the figures as far as possible. Cash actually in the cash box should equal the cash received less the cash paid out, after allowing for the starting balance of course. The balance on the bank statement should equal money banked less cheques written, after allowing for the opening balance and items that have not yet reached the statement.

Records kept in this way have severe limitations. Among them are:

- An item written down wrongly may not be noticed as a mistake
- Money owing to the organisation or by the organisation is not shown. The tennis club accounts will not show subscriptions not paid by members, or the amount owing to a painter for painting the clubhouse

- Long-term assets are not shown: £1 000 spent on tennis nets last year is not shown in this year's accounts

The concept of double entry bookkeeping

The concept and principles of double entry bookkeeping were first written down in 1494 by an Italian named Pacioli. His work has stood the test of time for the same principles are still valid today.

At the heart of double entry bookkeeping is the concept that every transaction involves the giving of a benefit and the receiving of a benefit. Consequently, every transaction is written into the books twice, once as a credit and once as a debit.

It follows from this that the bookkeeping system must balance, which is an enormous advantage for control purposes. The total of the debits must equal the total of the credits.

A set of double entry books enables a complete view to be taken, unlike a single entry system. For example, consider a businessman writing out a cheque for £100 wages. In a single entry system the only information recorded is that £100 wages has been paid. A double entry system also records that £100 has been taken from the bank account and that the bank account balance is reduced accordingly. This is extremely important information.

The basic rules and disciplines of double entry bookkeeping

A ledger or account is ruled for posting on two sides. Young trainee accountants are customarily told on their first morning that debit is nearest the window. This is of course not always true, but it is if they work with their left shoulders to the glass. Here is the first rule:

1 Debit on the left. Credit on the right
Computerised records are not likely to be printed in this traditional way. You are more likely to get a printout showing columns of figures. Some of these figures represent credits and some represent debits. They could be rewritten in the traditional format, and the debits would go on the left.

2 For every debit there must be a credit
This too is customarily told to trainee accountants on their first morning. Unlike the advice about windows this rule is infallible. There are no exceptions. Let us return to the businessman writing out a cheque for £100 wages. The entries are:

| Wages account | £100.00 debit |
| Bank account | £100.00 credit |

The entries may be numerous and complicated, but the rule still holds. If it is not followed the trial balance will not balance. A mistake has been made which must be found and corrected. Let us take the businessman purchasing £100 stationery which carries 17½% recoverable VAT. The entries are:

Stationery account	£100.00 debit
VAT account	£17.50 debit
Bank account	£117.50 credit

Scientists sometimes help themselves remember the rule by thinking of the law of physics 'for every action there is an equal and opposite reaction.'

3 Debit receives the benefit. Credit gives the benefit
This may be very hard to grasp and it is probably the opposite of what you would instinctively expect. After all your bank statement is credited when it receives money paid in. Nevertheless, double entry bookkeeping does work in this way. An account is debited when it receives a benefit and it is credited when it gives a benefit.

Consider yet again the businessman writing out a cheque for £100 wages. The worker receives the money and it is the wages account that is debited. The bank account gives the benefit and as a result has less money in it. Consequently, the bank account is credited.

It may help you to remember the rule if you think that a bank overdraft is represented by a credit balance in the bookkeeping system.

For another example we will take a sale of £200 to Smith and Sons. If it is a cash sale the entry is:

Bank account	£200.00 debit
Sales account	£200.00 credit

Money has been paid into the bank and the bank account is debited. If it is a sale on credit the entry is:

Smith and Sons	£200.00 debit
Sales account	£200.00 credit

When Smith and Sons actually pay, the entry is:

Bank account	£200.00 debit
Smith and Sons	£200.00 credit

The best way of understanding the basic principles is to work through examples and two examples follow. In the first case the correct entries follow immediately. In the second case just the account headings are given. You should fill in the entries before checking the correct postings which are given at the end of this chapter.

Samantha Jones runs a ladies dress shop. On one day the following financial events occur:

- She banks cash takings of £460
- She makes a credit sale of £100 to Mrs Clarke
- She purchases dresses from London Dress Supplies for £1 000. This is on credit
- She pays wages of £110
- Mrs Clarke pays £80 owing from a previous sale. This is banked

Bank account

Debit	£	Credit	£
Sales account	460	Wages account	110
Mrs Clarke account	80		

Sales account

Debit	£	Credit	£
		Bank account	460
		Mrs Clarke account	100

Mrs Clarke account

Debit	£	Credit	£
Sales account	100	Bank account	80

Stock account

Debit	£	Credit	£
London Dress Supplies account	1 000		

London Dress Supplies account

Debit	£	Credit	£
		Stock account	1 000

Wages account

Debit	£	Credit	£
Bank account	110		

The layout of the accounts has been simplified because it is only the principles of posting that are being illustrated. In real life, each entry would be dated and the balance of each account would be shown. Note that the total of all the debits equals the total of all the credits, £1750 in each case.

Now for the second example. Enter the entries on the blank accounts before checking the answers at the end of today's work, just after the Summary.

Peter Jenkins commences business as a manufacturer of pencils.

- He pays £50 000 into the bank as his capital for the business
- He buys plant and machinery for £20 000 from King Brothers Ltd. This is on credit
- He buys raw materials from Patel Brothers for £10 000. This is on credit
- He buys raw materials for £6 000 for cash
- He pays his lawyer £2 000 for negotiating a lease

Bank account

Debit		Credit
£		£

Capital account

Debit		Credit
£		£

Plant and Machinery account

Debit		Credit
£		£

King Brothers Ltd account

Debit		Credit
£		£

Patel Brothers Ltd account

Debit		Credit
£		£

Raw Materials account

Debit		Credit
£		£

Legal and Professional account

Debit		Credit
£		£

Summary

Today we have:

- Looked at single entry records and seen the drawbacks
- Established what is meant by double entry, and seen the advantages
- Seen that the giving and receiving of a benefit is at the heart of double entry bookkeeping
- Looked at basic rules and principles
- Worked through two examples

Tomorrow we will establish the five different types of accounts. We will also examine the different ledgers and day books.

Answers

p.13

Bank account

Debit	£		Credit	£
Capital account	50 000	Raw materials account		6 000
		Legal and professional account		2 000

Capital account

Debit	£		Credit	£
		Bank account		50 000

Plant and Machinery account

Debit			Credit
	£		£
King Brothers Ltd account	20 000		

King Brothers Ltd account

Debit		Credit	
	£		£
		Plant and machinery account	20 000

Patel Brothers Ltd account

Debit		Credit	
	£		£
		Raw materials account	10 000

Raw Materials account

Debit			Credit
	£		£
Patel Brothers Ltd account	10 000		
Bank account	6 000		

Legal and Professional account

Debit			Credit
	£		£
Bank account	2 000		

Different types of account and different ledgers

The rules for posting between accounts follow the rules of double entry bookkeeping and they do not vary according to the types of account involved. However, different types of account fulfil different purposes. They are treated differently when the profit and loss account and balance sheet are prepared. We start today by looking at the five different types of account.

We then progress to an examination of the nominal ledger, together with the subsidiary ledgers and the books of entry. The programme is:

- The five different types of account
- The nominal ledger
- The sales ledger
- The sales day book
- The purchase ledger
- The purchases day book

The five different types of account

It will be helpful for you to have an understanding of the
different types of account. This is in order to understand the
books and it is very important when accounts are prepared.
We will see this later in the week. However, it does not
affect the bookkeeping, and postings may freely be made
from one type of account to another.

Income accounts
These accounts relate to sales and they increase the profit.
The income accounts normally have a credit balance and are
eventually credited to the profit and loss account. An
example is the sales account into which Samantha Jones
credited £460 in Sunday's first example.

Expenditure accounts
These accounts are made up of expenditure that reduces
profit. The expenditure accounts normally have a debit
balance and are eventually debited to the profit and loss
account. An example of an expenditure account is the wages
account with a £110 balance from Sunday's first example.

Asset accounts
These accounts normally have a debit balance and are made
up of assets that retain their value. This is distinct from say
the electricity account which is an expenditure account.
Examples of asset accounts are stock, motor vehicles, and
bank accounts (if there is not an overdraft). Money owing to
the business is in debtor accounts and these are asset
accounts. An example is Mrs Clarke's account in Sunday's
first example. Asset accounts go into the balance sheet, not
the profit and loss account.

Liability accounts

These accounts are the debts of the business and they normally have a credit balance.

They eventually go into the balance sheet, not the profit and loss account. Examples are the accounts for money owing to suppliers and these accounts are called creditors. A further example is the bank account if there is an overdraft.

Capital accounts

These accounts represent the investment in the business by the owners. If the business is a company, it is the net worth owned by the shareholders. If you refer back to Sunday's second example you will see that Peter Jenkins started off his business by paying in £50 000, and that this was credited to a capital account. If the business makes profits the value of the capital accounts will increase in time.

So long as a business is solvent the capital accounts will have credit balances. If a business is not solvent the capital accounts will have debit balances. This is a desperate sign of trouble and often means that the closing of the business is imminent.

Now test your understanding of the types of account by classifying the following list. The answers are given at the end of the chapter but write them down before checking. Write the type of account and whether the balances are normally debit or credit.

1 Fixtures and fittings account
2 Salaries account
3 Legal and professional expenses account
4 Revenue reserves account

5 Share capital account
6 Trade debtors account
7 Trade creditors account
8 Hire purchase creditors account
9 Shop takings account
10 Goods sold account

The nominal ledger

The nominal ledger is the principal ledger. If other ledgers are kept they reconcile to a control account within the nominal ledger.

In very simple accounting systems only one ledger is maintained (the nominal ledger) and every single account is part of this main ledger. If there are say 10 customers, each one has an account within the nominal ledger. This option is open to all but it is only practical in the case of small and simple systems. Sheer numbers often necessitate the keeping of subsidiary sales and purchase ledgers. The detailed sales and purchase ledgers each reconcile to their own control account within the nominal ledger. According to circumstances other subsidiary ledgers may be kept. An example is a listing of the various fixed asset accounts.

The nominal ledger may be very big, perhaps containing thousands of individual accounts. This will certainly be the case for a major company and it is therefore necessary to have a system for coding and grouping the accounts.

In a simple system the accounts will just be listed, probably in alphabetical order. In a more complex system they will be grouped in a logical manner. For example, if there are several different bank accounts they may be listed next to each other. This is convenient, and when the balance sheet is prepared, all the bank accounts will be added to the one total that will appear in it. Similarly, it is usual to group all the overhead expenditure accounts by department.

In all but the very smallest systems, it is normal to give each account an identifying number. This is quicker to write out and if the system is mechanised or computerised, the person posting the entries will post according to the numbers only.

There are thousands of different accounting numbering systems and you may want to design your own to fit your business and individual circumstances. It is worth looking at the numbering system of your employer or some other organisation. Whether or not it is a good system, make sure that you understand the principles of the numbering.

The sales ledger

If your business is the making of nuclear bombs it is probable that you will have only one customer. I hope that there is only one and I hope that it is Her Majesty's Government! In this case, you will not need a detailed sales ledger, just one account in the nominal ledger. Nor will you need a sales ledger if your sales are entirely for cash.

On the other hand, businesses that sell on credit may have many customers. For them, an efficient sales ledger outside the nominal ledger is essential.

A sales ledger account looks very like a nominal ledger account. It is divided in the middle with debit on the left and credit on the right. There will be one account for each customer and the postings to it are:

debit   invoices issued
credit   credit notes issued
credit   cash received
credit   invoices written off as bad debts

Normally the debits on each account will exceed the credits. This means that the account has a debit balance which is the amount owed to the business by the customer. The total of the balances of all the sales ledger accounts is equal to the total amount owed to the business by the customers. This sum is represented by just one account (usually called the sales ledger control account) in the nominal system.

The bookkeeping system is designed to ensure that the accounts in the sales ledger do actually add up to the balance of the control account. This is explained shortly.

Sales ledger accounts ruled in the traditional way described may not be encountered too often, though they are still used extensively for small businesses. Many readers will only be familiar with computer printouts that do not look anything like the ledgers described. It is important to remember that a computer is just an efficient way of doing what could be done manually.

Some of the figures on the computer printout represent credits and some represent debits. They are just presented differently. It is worth proving this to yourself by marking the debits and credits on a computerised sales ledger.

A business needs to send out statements and operate credit control procedures. These are a by-product of the sales ledgers and a computerised system speeds up the process. A computerised system may operate on the open item principle. This means that cash payments are allocated to specific invoices, and customer statements only show unpaid invoices. A computerised system may readily give useful management information such as an ageing of the debts.

The sales day book

It is necessary to have a mechanism for posting sales invoices into the sales ledger and the nominal ledger. This could be done laboriously one by one, but it is better to group them together and cut down the work.

This posting medium is usually called the sales day book, though you might find it called the sales journal or some other name. The following is a typical example of a sales day book. However, the design can vary according to individual preference and business circumstances.

Date	Customer	Invoice no.	Folio no.	Goods total £	VAT £	Invoice total £
June 1	Bigg and Son	1001	B4	100.00	17.50	117.50
June 4	Carter Ltd	1002	C1	200.00	35.00	235.00
June 12	XYZ Ltd	1003	X1	50.00	8.75	58.75
June 17	Martin Bros	1004	M2	100.00	17.50	117.50
June 26	Fishers Ltd	1005	F5	10.00	1.75	11.75
June 30	Dawson Ltd	1006	D2	20.00	3.50	23.50
				480.00	84.00	564.00

Please note the following about each column:

- *Date*   This is the date of each individual invoice
- *Customer*   This is the customer to whom each individual invoice is addressed
- *Invoice No.*   Each invoice must be individually numbered
- *Folio No.*   This is the identifying code to each individual sales ledger account

- *Goods total* This is the total value of each invoice excluding VAT. Sometimes this is further divided to include different totals for different product groups. The example given only shows total sales
- *VAT* This is the VAT charged on each individual invoice
- *Invoice total* This is the total amount of each individual invoice and the amount that the customer has to pay

The columns may be added and the posting done whenever it is convenient to do so. Monthly posting is frequently encountered and in practice there would probably be more than six invoices. The posting to the nominal ledger would be:

Sales account	£480.00 credit	The sales account will eventually contribute to profit in the profit and loss account.
VAT account	£84.00 credit	This is a liability account. It is money owed by the business to the government.
Sales ledger control account	£564.00 debit	This is an asset account. It is money owing to the business by customers.

Six individual sales ledger accounts are debited with the total amount of the six individual invoices. You will notice that the balances of the sales ledger accounts will add up to the value of the sales ledger control account in the nominal system.

If you have a computerised system, your records will probably not look like this example. The computer will follow exactly these principles and do the same job, but it will do it more quickly.

The purchase ledger

If you have thoroughly understood the section on the sales ledger you will have no trouble at all understanding this section on the purchase ledger. This is because the purchase ledger is a mirror image of the sales ledger. It is used for invoices submitted to the business by suppliers.

The layout is similar to the accounts in the nominal ledger and the sales ledger. Postings to it are:

    credit   suppliers' invoices received
    debit   suppliers' credit notes received
    debit   cash payments made

Each account will normally have a credit balance and this represents the amount owing to the supplier by the business. The total of all the individual purchase ledger accounts is the same as the amount of the purchase ledger control account in the nominal ledger. Customers will submit statements to you and press you to make regular prompt payments to them.

The purchases day book

We have already seen that the purchase ledger is a mirror image of the sales ledger. You will therefore not be surprised to learn that the purchases day book is a mirror image of the sales day book. Do not be confused if you find it called the purchases journal or some other name, and do not be confused if it is a computerised system with a layout that makes sense to computer experts.

A typical purchase day book looks like the following:

Date	Customer	Invoice no.	Folio no.	Goods total £	VAT £	Invoice total £
July 1	Jones Ltd	3001	J8	100.00	17.50	117.50
July 9	King and Co	3002	K3	300.00	52.50	352.50
July 13	ABC Ltd	3003	A1	50.00	8.75	58.75
July 20	Dodd & Carr	3004	D2	200.00	35.00	235.00
July 28	Sugar Co Ltd	3005	S8	30.00	5.25	35.25
				680.00	119.00	799.00

The purchases day book is the medium through which a batch of suppliers' invoices is posted into the nominal system and into the purchase ledger. It avoids the need to enter them individually into the nominal system. It is usually ruled off and entered monthly but this can be done at any suitable interval.

Now test your understanding by writing down the three nominal posting entries resulting from the above purchases day book. Also write down the balance of Jones Ltd in the purchase ledger. The answers are given at the end of the chapter.

Summary

Today we have:

- Understood the five different types of nominal accounts and the differences between them
- Had a detailed look at the nominal ledger
- Had a detailed look at the sales ledger
- Had a detailed look at the sales day book
- Had a detailed look at the purchase ledger
- Had a detailed look at the purchases day book

Tomorrow we will continue our study of different aspects of bookkeeping

Answers
p.19

1	Assets account	normally debit balance
2	Expenditure account	normally debit balance
3	Expenditure account	normally debit balance
4	Capital account	normally credit balance
5	Capital account	normally credit balance
6	Assets account	normally debit balance
7	Liabilities account	normally credit balance
8	Liabilities account	normally credit balance
9	Income account	normally credit balance
10	Income account	normally credit balance

p.28

Nominal postings are:

Purchases account	£680.00 debit
VAT account	£119.00 debit
Purchase ledger control account	£799.00 credit

In practice the £680.00 would probably be spread over several different purchases account.

Jones Ltd will have a credit balance of £117.50 in the purchase ledger.

More aspects of bookkeeping

The programme today is deep and varied. You will study several more aspects of bookkeeping and attempt two practical examples.

- The cash book
- The bank reconciliation
- Other reconciliations and checks
- The journal
- Petty cash
- The trial balance

The cash book

Almost any set of accounting records involves the receiving and paying out of money. If there are only a few entries it may all be recorded in the bank account and cash account in the nominal ledger. However, due to the number of entries it is usual to maintain a separate cash book. Sometimes bank and cash are combined in one book and sometimes two books are kept. Today's work assumes that two books are kept.

Sometimes the 'cash book' is really a posting medium to the appropriate nominal ledger account. In this respect it is rather like the day books studied yesterday. The 'cash book' will have two sides, one for payments and one for receipts. The payments side would probably look like the following:

Date	Cheque no.	Payee	Folio	Amount £
May 4	1234	Simpson and Co.	S3	200.68
May 9	1235	Jones Ltd	J8	33.11
May 14	–	Bank charges	39	10.00
May 17	1236	Wainrights	W1	111.00
May 19	1237	Cubitt Ltd	C9	44.00
				398.79

The total of £398.79 would be credited to the bank account in the nominal ledger (remember payments out of a bank account are credits). Various accounts are debited and these are identified by the folio numbers.

In reality there may be hundreds of entries. The posting may be made easier by analysing the payment amount over extra columns. If there are three entries for bank charges only the total of the bank charges need be posted, rather than three individual items.

Sometimes the cash book is treated as a part of the nominal ledger not just as the posting medium to it. The following is an example of a full cash book balanced at the month end.

Receipts Date		Folio	Amount £	Date			Folio	Payments Amount £
Sept. 1	Balance	b/d	800.00	Sept. 1	4001	Arkwright	PL3	29.16
Sept. 4	Cross and Co.	SL6	101.10	Sept. 2	4002	Rates	NL4	290.00
Sept. 9	Figg Ltd	SL12	17.11	Sept. 6	4003	Stevens Ltd	PL7	34.12
Sept. 13	Morgan Ltd	SL17	34.19	Sept. 9	4004	Wilson Bros	PL19	47.11
Sept. 18	Peters and Brown	SL3	700.00	Sept. 12	4005	Crabbe and Co.	PL8	39.12
Sept. 30	Trapp Ltd	SL22	1 091.00	Sept. 17	4006	Carter	PL2	200.00
				Sept. 19	4007	Jenkins	PL12	56.99
				Sept. 23	4008	Champion and Co.	PL17	450.00
				Sept. 24	4009	Wages	NL4	290.00
				Sept. 29	4010	Barton and Hicks	PL1	300.00
				Sept. 30		Balance	c/d	1 006.90
			2 743.40					2 743.40
Oct. 1	Balance	b/d	1 006.90					

This is a completed cash book for the month of September. You will have noticed that the book has been ruled off and balanced, the first time this week that you have seen this done. The balancing may be done at any time but once a month is typical.

The balancing is done by adding the columns and writing in the difference on the side that has the smaller of the two figures. This is expressed as the balance carried down. The two columns then add to the same amount. The balancing figure is then transferred to the other column and becomes the opening balance in the next period.

In the example the balance brought down on September 1st is on the receipts side which means that there is money in the bank and no overdraft. This is still the position when the account is balanced on September 30th.

The four figure numbers before the names on the payments side are cheque numbers. This is optional and will assist when the bank reconciliation is done.

The bank reconciliation

The writer Ernest Hemingway often did not bother to bank cheques that he received, preferring instead to use them as bookmarks. After his death his house was found to contain dozens of unbanked cheques, some as much as 20 years old. This is an extreme example of one reason why the bank statement balance might not be the same as the cash book balance, and why it is necessary to reconcile the two balances.

It is good practice to write up the cash book frequently and to keep it up to date. That way you will know what the statement balance will be when all items reach the bank. You will have prior knowledge if the account is close to an overdraft or an agreed limit.

Possible reasons for a difference in the two figures are as follows:

- Cheques written in the cash book have not yet been debited to the bank statement
- Receipts written in the cash book have not yet been credited to the bank statement
- Items have been debited to the bank statement that have not yet been written in the cash book. Common examples are direct debits, standing orders and bank charges
- Receipts have been credited to the bank statement that have not yet been written in the cash book. This could for example be a credit transfer payment by a customer

> • You have made a mistake, perhaps the wrong
>   amount has been written into the cash book or a
>   paying-in slip has been added incorrectly
> • The bank has made a mistake. This is unlikely, but
>   it can happen

You should now be able to have a go at doing a bank
reconciliation. The following is a simplified bank statement
for the company whose cash book was given earlier in
today's work. It is for September, corresponding with the
period covered by the cash book. As it is a bank statement,
receipts are printed on the right, the opposite side to the
normal cash book layout.

Date	Detail	Payments £	Receipts £	Balance £
Sept 1	Opening balance			800.00 cr
Sept 6	Counter credit		101.10	
Sept 6	4001	29.16		
Sept 6	4002	290.00		581.94 cr
Sept 11	Counter credit		17.11	599.05 cr
Sept 12	Standing order - rates	105.16		493.89 cr
Sept 15	Counter credit		34.19	
Sept 15	4003	34.12		
Sept 15	4004	47.11		
Sept 15	Direct debit - water rates	61.82		385.03 cr
Sept 20	Counter credit		700.00	
Sept 20	Credit transfer received		349.21	1434.24 cr
Sept 21	4005	38.12		1396.12 cr
Sept 30	4008	450.00		946.12 cr

You must tick the bank statement to the cash book and
write out the differences. Do not worry about the best
layout, just have a go and write it down.

The answer is given at the end of today's work after the summary, but have a go before you check.

Other reconciliations and checks

If there is a bank account it should periodically be reconciled with the cash book or with the appropriate account in the nominal ledger. Furthermore, other accounts should periodically be reconciled or checked. One of these is petty cash and this is considered shortly.

From time to time, it should be checked that all the sales ledger accounts add up to the sales ledger control account in the nominal ledger. Similarly, all the purchase ledger accounts should add up to the purchase ledger control account in the nominal ledger.

If you have any sort of suspense account it is important that you analyse what items make up the balance. (A suspense account is, of course, an account where money is placed until a final accounting entry is decided.) I can reliably forecast that all sorts of nonsense will get dumped into the suspense account. I forecast this because it seems to happen to all suspense accounts. You must identify the items and take steps to clear them out. The list of potential reconciliations is a long one and it is good practice to reconcile where possible.

The journal

We have seen earlier this week that entries are made to the accounting records by means of the following books of entry:

- The sales day book
- The purchases day book
- The cash book

Entries are also made by means of the returns inwards book, the returns outwards book, and the petty cash book. The petty cash book is examined later today. The books of entry are completed by the journal and due to its importance it is explained in some detail now.

The journal is used to record important transactions that are not posted through the medium of any of the above books. You could just post the debits and credits to the right accounts without recording them in a book. Many bookkeepers do just this but it is much better to use the journal. This makes fraud and mistakes less likely, making it easier to check the books; and most importantly you have a narrative explanation for the entries. Auditors prefer the use of a journal.

The journal is ruled to show the date, a reference number for the entry, the identity and amount of the account to be credited, the identity and amount of the account to be debited, and a narrative explanation. An example of a journal entry is as follows:

		Debit	Credit
March 1st	Bad debts written off	£1 000.00	
JV99	Curzon & Co		£1 000.00

To write off bad debt following bankruptcy of customer

Petty cash

The word 'petty' means small or trivial, and the purpose of the petty cash system is to allow small and trivial disbursements to be made. This limitation may not always be apparent to colleagues who will try and obtain large sums of money from it. Nevertheless, the purpose is to handle small sums of money.

A typical petty cash book is very wide, has two sides, and has a considerable number of columns for analysis. This makes it difficult to reproduce here but the following is a simplified example of how the payments side typically looks.

Date	Details of expense	Voucher no.	Total £	Stamps £	Petrol £
May 2	Stamps	1	10.00	10.00	
May 16	Petrol	2	18.48		18.48
May 29	Stamps	3	10.00	10.00	
			38.48	20.00	18.48
May	Balance c/d		11.52		
			50.00		

In practice there would of course be many more entries and a further dozen or so analysis columns to record the different categories of expense (milk, stationery, etc.).

Note that the total column is always used and this is the total amount paid out on each voucher. If someone is claiming £10 for stamps and £10 for petrol then £20 would be entered in the total column.

The example assumes that the imprest system is in use and that the float is £50. The imprest system is loved by auditors and is much superior to other systems.

Under the imprest system the amount of money in the petty cash box, plus the payments made and recorded in the book, should add up to the amount of the float. If they do not, a mistake has been made. In the example on the previous page a cheque for £38.48. would be written and cashed. This would restore the float to £50 and this would be the opening balance for June. The accounting entries to record the May transactions would be:

Postage account	£20.00 debit
Petrol account	£18.48 debit
Petty cash account	£38.48 credit

The entry for the reimbursement cheque would be:

| Petty cash account | £38.48 debit |
| Bank account | £38.48 credit |

After all the entries have been posted, the petty cash account should have a balance of £50 debit in the nominal ledger. It is an asset account and there is £50 cash to support it. A £50 cheque would have been written on Day 1.

The trial balance

There are two very good reasons for taking out a trial balance. First, it is one of the steps towards preparing the profit and loss account and the balance sheet. Second, it is proof that, subject to certain exceptions described shortly, the books are in order. It is good practice to take out a trial balance regularly, perhaps once a month. This means that if there is a mistake to be found, only a month's entries need be checked.

Please note particularly the phrase 'take out the trial balance'. The trial balance is not an account and it does not involve posting. It is the listing of all the balances in the ledger. You will remember that for every debit there must be a credit. It follows that the total of all the debit balances must equal the total of all the credit balances. If they do not do so then a mistake has been made.

There are limitations to the proofs provided by a trial balance. It may balance and yet the following two types of errors will not be disclosed:

- A compensating error: this is two mistakes for the same amount, one increasing the debits and one increasing the credits
- The right amount posted to the wrong account

Both these types of errors are nasty and you may never realise that a mistake has been made. They mean that two accounts are wrong.

A difference on the trial balance will disclose one of the following mistakes:

- A mistake in listing or adding the trial balance
- A wrong addition on an account
- A mistake in writing out the brought forward balances
- One side of an entry not posted (double entry not complete)
- Posting of wrong amount
- A missing ledger sheet

You might find the cause of a trial balance difference by means of a random search. However, it is much better to conduct the search in a systematic manner. You *must* locate the cause of the difference if you do the following in a *systematic* way:

1 Check the listing of the balances within the trial balance
2 Check the addition of the trial balance

3 Check the listing of the opening balances. These are
   either the balances brought down or the balances at the
   time that the last trial balance was agreed
4 Check the addition of each individual account within
   the trial balance. Check from the brought forward
   balances or the balances making up the last trial
   balance
5 Tick each individual posting during the period under
   review. Every debit should have a matching credit and
   there should be no unticked entries at the end

If done properly this must find the difference.

We will finish today with an example of a trial balance, a
series of postings, and the new trial balance. The new trial
balance is given after the summary of today's work, but
prepare it for yourself before checking the answer.

Summarised trial balance

	Debit	**Credit**
	£	£
Capital account		50 000
Sales account		1 000 000
Sales ledger creditors		20 000
Cost of sales account	500 000	
Stock account	300 000	
Overhead account	190 000	
Bank account	80 000	
	1 070 000	1 070 000

Cash sales of £400 000 are made. Cost of sales is 50% of
sales. £300 000 is spent on overheads, half on credit and half
for cash. £600 000 fixed assets are purchased for cash.

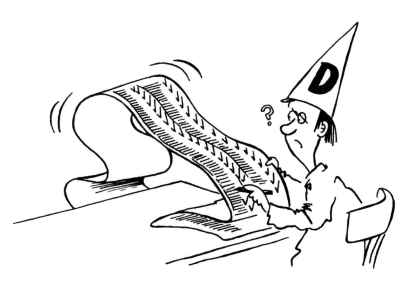

Summary

Today we have:

- Studied the layout and operation of the cash book and the postings from it
- Studied bank reconciliations and attempted an example
- Considered other reconciliations and checks
- Examined the journal
- Considered petty cash, especially the imprest system
- Examined trial balances and tried working from one trial balance through to another

Tomorrow we will look at how to prepare for the accounts.

Answers
p.35

Cash book balance at September 30th		1006.90 dr
Add cheques not yet presented:		
4006	200.00	
4007	56.99	
4009	290.00	
4010	300.00	
		846.99
		1853.89
Add credit on statement not in cash book		349.21
		2203.10
Less receipt in cash book not on statement		1091.10
		1112.10
Less payments on statement not in cash book		
Standing order – rates	105.16	
Direct debit – water rates	61.82	
		166.98
		945.12
Add difference to be investigated (cheque 4005 for £39.12 entered by bank as £38.12)		1.00
As per bank statement balance at September 30th		946.12 dr

This is not easy, so congratulations if you got it right. It does illustrate all the principles effectively.

p.42

	Debit £	Credit £
Capital account		50 000
Sales account		1 400 000
Sales ledger creditors		170 000
Cost of sales account	700 000	
Stock account	100 000	
Overhead accounts	490 000	
Bank account		270 000
Fixed asset accounts	600 000	
	1 890 000	1 890 000

Preparation for the accounts

We now turn to important accounting entries, not yet recorded in the trial balance, but which are vital to the preparation of accurate accounts. We then conclude today's work by seeing how the trial balance is adjusted to reflect these entries. The programme is:

- Accruals
- Prepayments
- Reserves and provisions
- Depreciation
- Posting final adjustments and the extended trial balance

Accruals

We concluded yesterday's work by considering the trial balance. This should accurately reflect the position after posting all the entries. But what about charges that have not yet been put into the accounts? Sometimes a supplier may be late submitting an invoice. If you work in a large accounts office you will know that an occasional invoice may be submitted a year or more after the event.

Furthermore, suppliers' invoices may be lost or held up pending approval. The more quickly the books are closed off after the end of the accounting period, the more numerous will be the invoices not entered.

These problems can be overcome by entering what are called accruals. These are calculated in one of two ways:

1 A specific invoice received after the close off. If the electricity bill to March 31st is £1 507.46 and accounts are done for the year to March 31st, then you will accrue either £1 507 or £1 500. It would be most unusual to bother with pence

2 An informed estimate. If the electricity bill averages £1 000 a quarter, and the last bill is up to March 15th, it would be reasonable to accrue £170 at March 31st. It is usual for most accruals to be informed estimates.

Accruals are costs incurred but not yet entered. The accounting entry is to debit the account of the expense (e.g. electricity) and to credit accruals account. The accruals account is a liability account because it is money owing by the business.

Prepayments

A prepayment is the exact opposite of an accrual which is a cost incurred but not yet entered. A prepayment is a cost entered but not yet incurred.

A prepayment may be necessary because a supplier has raised an invoice early, or because you have left the books open to catch as many invoices as possible and one from the next period has slipped through. For example an invoice dated July 3rd may slip through if you make the accounts up to June 30th, but leave the books open for two weeks beyond that date.

More usually, a prepayment may be necessary because an invoice has been entered that covers a benefit to be received in the future. A very common example is insurance which may be paid a year in advance.

We will consider an insurance invoice for £12 000 that has been paid on December 31st, and which pays for insurance cover over the following 12 months. Let us assume that the business prepared its accounts at June 30th. Obviously, unless an adjustment is made, overheads will be too large and the profit will be too small.

The answer is to prepay six twelfths of £12 000 which equals £6 000. Insurance (an overhead account) is credited with £6 000 and prepayments account is debited £6 000. The prepayments account is an asset account because it is money paid in advance for goods and services. It is like the deposit that you may pay in February for your summer holiday to be taken in August.

You may well now be asking what eventually happens to the entries for accruals and prepayments after the accounts have been prepared. The answer is that they are reversed. This is explained later today.

You should now take a few moments to test your understanding by writing down the entries for the following. The answers are given at the end of today.

A local authority staff restaurant prepares accounts at May 31st

- £70 invoice for bread from the wholesalers dated June 8th has been entered into the books
- The telephone account for the quarter to March 31st was £600. No later invoice has been received
- Six months water rates in advance totalling £900 were paid on March 31st
- Food with a total value of £700 was delivered to the canteen on May 29th. No invoice has been received
- Wages average £350 a week and are paid weekly in arrears. Payment has been made for work done up to May 26th (a seven-day week is worked)

Reserves and provisions

On Monday you read that reserves were part of the capital of a business and represented money belonging to the shareholders or other owners. However, the term has a very different meaning as well.

Reserves are made to cover an event that may well happen (or has actually happened) but which is not adequately recorded in the books. Provisions are very similar and in practice the two terms are almost interchangeable.

A bad debt reserve is an easily understood example. Company A made a credit sale of £100 000 to Company B. The entries in the books of Company A were:

Sales account	£100 000 credit
Trade debtors account	£100 000 debit

Good news so far. The balance of the sales account will eventually be credited to the profit and loss account and will increase profit. It is expected that Company B will soon send a cheque for £100 000 to clear the trade debtors account. But Company B's chairman is arrested and charged with fraud, the directors resign, the company goes into liquidation, and the liquidator forecasts an eventual dividend of 10p in the pound to unsecured creditors.

To put it mildly, the books of Company A do not reflect the true position. They overstate the true profit by £90 000. Company A will need the following entry in its books:

Bad debt reserve account	£90 000 credit
Bad debt account	£90 000 debit

The bad debts account is a charge to the profit and loss account. This reduces the £100 000 sale contribution to a realistic £10 000.

The bad debt reserve account is placed against trade debtors account in the balance sheet. It is thus reduced to £10 000 which is the amount expected to be eventually paid.

Bad debt reserves may be against specific debts as above, or they may be a realistic general reserve. A major book club sells books to the public by post and sends out the books before payment is made. At any one time it is owed money by many thousands of different customers. Each debt is individually small. Experience may show that a bad debt reserve of say 5% of the total outstanding is necessary.

Reserves and provisions are necessary for more than just bad debts. The list is very long and you may well be able to think of some circumstances that relate to a business with which you are familiar. The following are just some of the possibilities.

- Provision for settlement discounts payable. Suppose that your business offers 5% settlement discount to all customers who pay within 30 days of invoice date. Unless you make a provision you will overstate the profits. Not all customers will take advantage of the settlement discount so perhaps a provision of 4% of the total sum outstanding would be realistic
- Provision for fulfilling warranty claim obligations. Suppose that you supply double-glazed windows and guarantee to repair faulty workmanship free of charge for up to 10 years after installation. A realistic provision for the cost of future repairs would be necessary
- Provision for settlement of outstanding legal claims. These could be for alleged negligence, faulty workmanship, wrongful dismissal, libel, or many other matters. Again, a realistic estimate of the eventual cost should be provided.
- Provision for losses on a contract or joint venture. Perhaps one of these has gone wrong. Your organisation has a legal obligation to complete the work, but it is clear that at the end a loss will be made. Provision should be made for the loss as soon as it can realistically be foreseen. You should not wait to charge the profit and loss account in future years

In all cases the accounting entry is:

> Credit a suitably named reserve or provision account
> Debit the appropriate account in the profit and loss section

Depreciation

Current assets are assets with a value available to the business in the short term, usually taken to mean up to a year. Examples are cash, stock, and trade debtors (money owing by customers). Fixed assets are assets with a value available in the long term, usually taken to mean more than a year. Examples are motor vehicles, leases, plant and machinery, and computer equipment.

Some fixed assets hold their value indefinitely, but most do not. The value of most fixed assets diminishes either with time (e.g. leases), with wear and tear (e.g. plant and equipment), or both (e.g. motor cars).

Perhaps the simplest example of this is a lease. Take leasehold property purchased for £300 000, and with 10 years of the lease remaining. On the day that the property is purchased it is worth £300 000. Ten years later it is worth nothing. Its value reduced by £30 000 each year. If the accounts do not recognise this, both the profit and the value of the assets are overstated.

It is therefore necessary to write off most fixed assets over a period of time. A formula must be found that fairly reflects the reduction in value. In the case of the £300 000 lease the annual bookkeeping entry is:

Depreciation account	£30 000 debit
Leasehold property account	£30 000 credit

The depreciation account is a profit and loss account item and reduces the profit. The credit to the leasehold property account reduces the value of the asset which you will remember is a debit balance. This is the straight-line method of depreciation which is the most common and the simplest. It involves writing off an equal amount over a fixed number of years.

Another common method is the depreciating balance method. This writes off a given percentage of the remaining balance. A feature of this method is that the value of the asset in the books can never quite reach zero. This is usually realistic; after all even a 20-year-old motor car is worth something.

An example of this is an item of machinery purchased for £100 000 and written off at 25% per year on the reducing balance method. The depreciation charge will be as follows:

Year 1	25% x £100 000	= £25 000
Year 2	25% x £75 000	= £18 750
Year 3	25% x £56 250	= £14 063

There are other methods as well. Care must be taken to choose an appropriate depreciation policy and it must be applied consistently from year to year.

Posting final adjustments and the extended trial balance

We finish today's work by considering how the trial balance is finalised for the preparation of the accounts. Yesterday, we saw that the production of the trial balance is a key stage in the preparation of accounts. If the accounts are very simple, and everything up to date, there may not be any further entries to post. In these cases the accountant can proceed directly to prepare the accounts. We will look at accounts preparation in detail on Thursday and Friday.

This though is unusual, especially if there are a lot of entries. It is usually necessary to list the trial balance, open the accounts for the next period, then work through a list of adjustments to the trial balance. There are nearly always accruals and prepayments. There are often reserves and provisions to enter, mistakes to be corrected, and there may be many other adjustments as well.

There are two basic approaches for posting the adjustments which we will consider in turn:

1   *Actually posting the entries*
All the adjustments are posted in the ledgers and then a new trial balance is listed. This new trial balance is used to prepare the accounts. All the adjustment entries are then reverse posted into the ledgers in the next period. This reverse posting is necessary because the ledgers have to be restored to the position before the adjustments.

This may be difficult to understand but consider an accrual of £1 000 for a late telephone bill. The accrual is a debit to the overhead account. In the next period the reverse posting puts a credit of £1 000 into the overhead account. When the actual invoice for £1 000 arrives it is a debit and cancels out the credit leaving a nil balance. This is correct because it was a late invoice which should affect only profit only in the earlier period.

Computerised accounting systems usually operate in this way. This is because it is relatively simple for the computer to be programmed to reverse post automatically into the following period.

2   *The extended trial balance*
The second approach is to list all the adjustments into extra columns to the trial balance (one debit column and one credit column). The trial balance is then repeated taking account of the adjustments. The whole thing is on one piece of paper and there are six columns in total (sometimes eight columns but we will not bother with this). It is extremely

important that all the adjustments are properly cross-referenced to a full list of the changes and a narrative explanation of them.

We will conclude today by looking at an extended trial balance for Bridget Murphy who is a public relations consultant. She commences business on July 1st and the extended trial balance is at the end of her first year in business on the following June 30th. Note that the title and date should be given at the top.

The extended trial balance is given over the page and you should study it carefully. It incorporates adjustments to reflect the following:

- Motor vehicle and office equipment should both be depreciated by 25%
- Bridget has not yet entered an invoice for £5 000 for work that she has done
- Bank interest to June 30th not yet entered into the books is £2 643
- On May 21st Bridget paid £2 400 insurance to cover a year in advance
- Bridget has received invoices as follows but not entered them into the books:
    - Office expenses   £1 800
    - Travel expenses   £ 246
    - Stationery   £ 679
- Her telephone account averages £1 800 a quarter and she has paid the bill up to May 31st
- Bridget believes that £10 000 owing to her will turn out to be a bad debt

	Opening Trial Balance		Adjustments		Closing Trial Balance	
	Debit £	Credit £	Debit £	Credit £	Debit £	Credit £
Motor vehicles	20 000.00				20 000.00	
Office equipment	15 000.00				15 000.00	
Depreciation of motor vehicle				5 000.00		5 000.00
Depreciation of office equipment				3 750.00		3 750.00
Bank account		23 185.16				23 185.16
Trade debtors	5 708.31		5 000.00		10 708.31	
Trade creditors		661.19				661.19
Reserve for bad debts				1 000.00		1 000.00
Accruals				5 968.00		5 968.00
Prepayments			2 400.00		2 400.00	
Fees invoiced		62 000.00		5 000.00		67 000.00
Salaries	12 000.00				12 000.00	
Insurance	4 600.00			2 400.00	2 200.00	
Office expenses	7 309.14		1 800.00		9 109.14	
Travel expenses	11 111.18		246.00		11 357.18	
Stationery	3 209.47		679.00		3 888.47	
Telephone	6 908.25		600.00		7 508.25	
Interest			2 643.00		2 643.00	
Bad debts			1 000.00		1 000.00	
Depreciation			8 750.00		8 750.00	
	85 846.35	85 846.35	23 118.00	23 118.00	106 564.35	106 564.35

Summary

Today we have examined some of the calculations that have to be made before the final accounts are prepared, and we have seen how these are incorporated into the trial balance. Specifically we have:

- Studied accruals and prepayments
- Tested our understanding of accruals and prepayments
- Studied reserves and provisions
- Studied depreciation
- Seen how the adjustments are entered into the accounts
- Studied the extended trial balance

Tomorrow, we move on to a detailed examination of the profit and loss account.

Answers

p 49

	Debit £	Credit £
Prepayments account	70	
Food purchased account		70
Accruals account		400
Telephone account	400	
Prepayments account	600	
Water rates account		600
Accruals account		700
Food purchased account	700	
Accruals account		250
Wages account	250	

The profit and loss account

During the first four days of the week we have worked through the principles of bookkeeping up to the extended trial balance. We are now ready to see the accounts resulting from the work. Today it is the profit and loss account, and the programme is:

- What is the profit and loss account?
- A straightforward profit and loss account
- A trading business
- A manufacturing business
- Two further important points

What is the profit and loss account?

The profit and loss account is a summary of all the revenue and expense items occurring in a specified period of time. The profit and loss account should be properly headed and the period of time stated.

The period is usually a year, especially in the case of published accounts, but other periods may be encountered. Internal profit statements prepared for management may be done weekly, monthly, quarterly or for some other convenient period. The selection of the period does matter. Consider a greetings card shop preparing a profit statement for the six months to August 31st. Twenty-five per cent of a year's turnover comes in the five weeks ending on December 24th.

The bookkeeping procedure is:

1 Make sure that everything is posted up to date
2 Post all the final adjustments. This was explained yesterday
3 List the final adjusted trial balance
4 Extract the revenue and expense accounts and list these separately. If the credit balances exceed the debit balances there is a profit. If the debit balances are greater there is a loss
5 Open the ledger for the next period. All the revenue and expense accounts will be opened with a nil balance. The net profit or net loss will be transferred to the capital account, thus increasing or decreasing the amount of capital that the proprietor has invested in the business. This ensures that the trial balance continues to balance
6 The accruals and prepayments are reverse posted into the new period

A straightforward profit and loss account

There are more things to learn when goods are purchased for resale and stocks are held. A step beyond that is when manufacturing takes place. We will study all this later today, but first of all let us understand a straightforward profit and loss account. The examples are well illustrated with the figures for Bridget Murphy. She is the public relations consultant whose extended trial balance was listed yesterday.

Please refer back to that extended trial balance. You should be able to recognise which accounts are revenue and expense accounts. You should therefore be able to follow how her profit and loss account is extracted. It is given below.

Bridget Murphy

Profit and loss account for year to June 30th

	£	£
Fees invoiced		67 000
Less expenses:		
Salaries	12 000	
Insurance	2 200	
Office expenses	9 109	
Travel expenses	11 357	
Stationery	3 888	
Telephone	7 508	
Interest	2 643	
Bad debts	1 000	
Depreciation	8 750	
		58 455
Net Profit		8 545

You should now test your knowledge of the profit and loss account by preparing one. The answer is given at the end of the chapter but prepare the account before looking at the answer.

Bernard Smith starts work as a painter and decorator on June 1st. He does not hold stocks of materials as he buys just enough for each job. At the following May 31st his trial balance is as follows:

	Debit	Credit
	£	**£**
Motor van	6 000.00	
Ladder and tools	1 000.00	
Bank account	300.00	
Trade debtors	700.00	
Trade creditors		400.00
Invoiced sales		15 000.00
Materials used	2 000.00	
Motor expenses	1 400.00	
Other overhead costs	4 000.00	
	15 400.00	15 400.00

Bernard Smith is advised that he should depreciate the motor van by 25%, and the ladder and tools by 10%.

He believes that half the trade debtors are an irrecoverable bad debt. He holds an invoice for materials for £600 and an overheads invoice for £200. Neither have been entered into the books. He has paid £500 for a year's insurance in advance.

A customer has complained about bad workmanship. Bernard Smith has agreed to spend £200 putting it right.

A trading business

So far we have only considered businesses that do not hold stock. It is now time to see how the accounts deal with this problem.

You will, I hope, quickly see that the profit and loss account must only show the cost of the goods sold in the period. A wrong figure, perhaps a ridiculous figure, will be obtained if the cost of goods purchased in the period is used.

The cost of goods sold in the period is obtained in the following way.

- Take the value of stock at the beginning of the period
- Add purchases during the period
- Subtract the value of stock at the end of the period

The value of stock at the beginning and end of the period may be established by stocktaking. If financial controls are extremely good they may be calculated figures, with occasional stock checks to prove the system. If there has been any theft or other form of stock shrinkage, stock will be reduced and consequently the cost of sales will be increased. The principle is illustrated by the profit and loss account of a school tuck shop. There are no costs other than the cost of the food sold. The profit and loss account is given below.

Sales in the month of February total £430. Stock at January 31st was £100. Stock at February 28th was £120. Purchases in February were £380.

School tuck shop
Profit and loss account for February month

	£	£
Sales		430
Stock at January 31	100	
Add purchases in February	380	
	480	
Less stock at February 28th	120	
		360
Net profit		70

The same principles apply in the profit and loss accounts of Tesco and Marks and Spencer, although of course the figures are considerably bigger! These companies buy food and other products from their suppliers, they have stock checks at the beginning and end of each trading period (or they calculate the stock), and they sell to the public.

A manufacturing business

You have already seen that the profit and loss account of a trading company must only contain the costs of the goods actually sold. The cost of goods purchased and held in stock must be excluded. For the same reason the profit and loss account of a manufacturing company must only contain the manufacturing costs of the goods actually sold in the period. The manufacturing costs of goods not sold must be excluded.

As with a trading company it will probably be necessary to stocktake at the beginning and end of the period, but if controls are very good it may not always be necessary.

Sometimes the manufacturing costs are shown in a separate manufacturing account. This leads to a manufacturing profit which is carried forward to the profit and loss account. Other costs are deducted in the main profit and loss account to give the overall profit or loss. Similarly, trading activities are sometimes shown in a separate trading account. This method of presentation is optional and not followed here. We will show everything in the main profit and loss account.

Key points to remember:
- There are definite starting and finishing dates
- Total sales appear at the top
- The net profit or loss is at the bottom
- All revenue and expense accounts are included
- Only expenditure on goods actually sold is included

The principles are best shown with an example:

Bognor Cases Ltd manufactures and sells suitcases. Sales in the year to June 30th 1995 were £1 000 000. Purchases of raw materials and components in the year totalled £400 000. Stock at June 30th 1994 was £320 000 and at June 30th 1995 it was £365 000.

Wages of production staff were £216 000. Factory rent was £110 000 and factory power costs were £40 000. Other production costs were £40 000. Salaries of salesmen, administration staff and management totalled £82 000. Other overheads were £66 000.

Bognor Cases Ltd
Profit and loss account for year to June 30th 1995

	£	£
Sales		1 000 000
Stock at 30.6.94	320 000	
Add purchases	400 000	
	720 000	
Less stock at 30.6.95	365 000	
	355 000	
Production wages	216 000	
Factory rent	110 000	
Power costs	40 000	
Other production costs	40 000	
Cost of manufacturing		761 000
		239 000
Less overheads		
Salaries	82 000	
Other overheads	66 000	
		148 000
Net profit		91 000

Note that the costs are split into two sections. All costs relating to the product and manufacturing go into the top part. These contribute to the cost of manufacturing and to the subtotal which is the manufacturing profit. Overhead costs go below this subtotal.

You should find the following exercise quite easy. The answer is given at the end of the chapter but set it out before looking.

North West Garden Novelties Ltd manufactures and sells garden gnomes. Sales in the year to April 30th 1995 were £600 000.

Purchases of materials totalled £200 000. Stock at April 30th 1994 was £50 000 and stock at April 30th 1995 was £40 000.

Production wages in the year were £280 000 and other production costs were £90 000. Total overheads were £60 000.

Two further important points

To complete today's study of the profit and loss account we will consider two important concepts.

Cost must be matched to invoice
When we studied trading companies and manufacturing companies we saw that the costs of goods sold, and not of any other goods, should be brought into the account.

The same applies to all the costs, and an example of where it is particularly relevant is a long-term construction contract, such as the building of the Channel Tunnel. When 30% of the project is included in income, it is vital that costs exactly relating to this 30% are included.

Accounts should be prepared on a prudent basis
Again, construction projects are a good example. Profits should not be taken before they have been earned. A loss should be taken when it can be realistically foreseen, but a profit should only be taken when it has been earned.

Summary

This Thursday we have:

- Understood exactly what a profit and loss account is
- Studied a simple example
- Looked at trading businesses
- Looked at manufacturing businesses
- Briefly looked at two important concepts

Tomorrow we progress to the other main part of the accounts, the balance sheet.

Answers
p.63

Bernard Smith
Profit and loss account for year to May 31st

	£	£
Invoiced sales		15 000
Less Costs:		
Materials used	2 200	
Motor expenses	1 400	
Other overhead costs	3 700	
Depreciation	1 600	
Bad debt	350	
Remedial work	200	
		9 450
Net profit		5 550

p.69

North West Novelties Ltd
Profit and loss account for year to April 30th 1995

	£	£
Sales		600 000
Stock at 30.4.94	50 000	
Add purchases	200 000	
	250 000	
Less stock at 30.4.95	40 000	
	210 000	
Production wages	280 000	
Other production costs	90 000	
Cost of manufacturing		580 000
		20 000
Less total overheads		60 000
Net loss for year		(40 000)

This is the first time today that we have encountered a loss. Note that it is shown by means of a bracketed figure.

The balance sheet

The two main constituent parts of a set of accounts are the profit and loss account and the balance sheet. You should now be familiar with the principles of the profit and loss account so today we progress to the balance sheet. The programme is:

- What is a balance sheet?
- The concept of ownership
- The layout of the balance sheet
- The main balance sheet headings

What is a balance sheet?

You can help yourself remember the answer to this question by thinking of the literal meaning of the two words balance and sheet.

Balance This means that the balance sheet must balance. There are two sides to it and they must total to the same figure. Put another way, the sum of the debit balances must equal the sum of the credit balances; all the figures come from the extended trial balance.

Sheet This means literally a sheet of paper on which the figures are listed.

Earlier in the week we saw that there are five different types of account. Yesterday we saw that the revenue and expense accounts are extracted from the extended trial balance and that these accounts make up the profit and loss account. The balance sheet is made up from everything that is left. These are the three remaining types of account.

- Asset accounts   (debit balances)
- Liability accounts   (credit balances)
- Capital accounts   (normally credit balances)

The profit or loss at the bottom of the profit and loss account is added to, or subtracted from, the capital accounts. The result is that the balance sheet balances, which is essential. We saw yesterday that the profit and loss account covers a given period of time. If trading is continuing, the profit or loss would be different if the period were to be one day shorter or longer. The balance sheet is not like that. It is a listing of the balances on just one fixed date, very often the date at the end of the trading period.

The concept of ownership

Asset and liability accounts are relatively easy to understand, but you may have a problem understanding the capital accounts. Sometimes there is just one account called the capital account. In other cases, there may be several accounts: share capital account, revenue reserves account, and so on.

The capital accounts represent the money invested in the business by the owners. The owners are a different entity to the business itself. If the company is wound up, and if the assets and liabilities are worth exactly book value, the owners will be paid out exactly the value of the capital accounts.

This is easy to understand in the case of a public company. If you own shares in Barclays Bank plc you are not the same as the bank. The capital accounts in the books of Barclays Bank plc represent the debt owing to you and to the other shareholders.

The principle is exactly the same in the accounts of a one-man or one-woman business. Let us return yet again to Bridget Murphy the public relations consultant. Bridget Murphy the person is separate from Bridget Murphy the business. If she is efficient she will have two bank accounts, one for her business and one for her personal affairs. She may even pay herself a salary from one bank account to the other.

If Bridget Murphy's business is wound up, what is left after everything has been collected in and paid out, belongs to her. The final cheque in the cheque-book pays her the value of the capital accounts.

This is the reason that the capital accounts are listed with the liabilities.

The layout of the balance sheet

Until the last 30 years or so, it was the practice to set out the figures side by side. The liabilities (credit balances) were listed in the left-hand column, and the assets (debit balances) were listed in the right-hand column. The two columns, of course, added up to the same figure.

You may occasionally see a balance sheet set out like this, but it is now much more common to see balance sheets set out in a vertical format. The examples in this chapter are shown in the vertical format.

A vertical balance sheet shows liabilities deducted from assets in a logical manner. The whole thing adds down to the net worth of the business, which is shown at the bottom. This 'net worth' is represented by the capital accounts.

This is best illustrated with an example. There follows the balance sheet of a partnership where the two partners participate 50/50 in the profits.

Smith and Jones
Balance Sheet at April 30th 1995

Fixed assets	£	£
Freehold property	200 000	
Plant and machinery	120 000	
Motor vehicles	40 000	
		360 000
Current assets		
Stock	170 000	
Trade debtors	130 000	
	300 000	
Less current liabilities		
Bank overdraft	60 000	
Trade creditors	120 000	
	180 000	
Net current assets		120 000
		480 000
Capital accounts		
Smith		240 000
Jones		240 000
		480 000

This is, of course, a simple balance sheet. In practice there would be several notes giving relevant details of how the figures are made up. Note that the net worth of the partnership is £480 000. If the partnership were to be wound up, if the assets and liabilities achieved book value, and if there were no winding up expenses, Smith and Jones would get £240 000 each.

You should now prepare a balance sheet from the trial balance given below. The answer is given at the end of the chapter but prepare your answer before checking. The accounts are given in alphabetical order, not the order in which they appear in the balance sheet.

John Cohen
Trial balance at April 30th 1995

	Debit £	Credit £
Bank account	10 000	
Capital reserve		70 000
Depreciation on motor vehicle		30 000
Depreciation on plant and machinery		140 000
Leasehold property	100 000	
Motor vehicles	60 000	
Plant and machinery	280 000	
Revenue reserves		240 000
Stock	150 000	
Taxation		80 000
Trade creditors		200 000
Trade debtors	160 000	
	760 000	760 000

Taxation is money owing to the government by the business. Depreciation must be netted off against the relevant asset accounts. This means that the difference between the two figures is shown in the balance sheet.

The main balance sheet headings

Of course not every individual account in the trial balance appears individually in the balance sheet. If it did the balance sheet of a major company would have to be hundreds of pages long. The need for this is overcome by grouping accounts of a similar type. For example, there may be several types of fixed asset. They will appear in the balance sheet as just one total figure with further detail given in a suitable note.

The following explanations will help you understand the headings commonly used in balance sheets.

Fixed assets
These are assets whose use generates benefit to the business in the long term. This is usually taken to mean a year or more. Because of their fixed and long-term nature, they are grouped separately from current assets, whose value can be expected to be realised in the short term.

It is normally necessary to depreciate fixed assets and this was studied in detail earlier in the week. In practice, it is rare for fixed assets to be actually worth exactly their written down value in the books. The reasons are:

1   The arbitrary nature of the depreciation rules
2   Individual circumstances
3   Inflation

Examples of fixed assets are:

- Freehold property
- Leasehold property
- Plant and equipment
- Computers
- Fixtures and fittings
- Motor vehicles

Asset strippers specialise in finding companies where the fixed assets are actually worth more than the book value. They then purchase the company, unlock the value by selling some or all of the assets, and realising the profit.

Current assets

These are assets whose value is available to the business in the short term. This is either because they are part of the trading cycle (such as stock and trade debtors) or because they are short-term investments (such as a 90-day bank deposit account). The definition of 'short term' is usually taken to be less than a year.

Debtors are usually current assets. The definition of a debtor is a person owing money to the business, such as a customer for goods sold. Examples of current assets are:

- Stock
- Trade debtors
- Bank accounts
- Short-term investments

Current liabilities
These are liabilities which the business could be called upon
to pay off in the short term. Examples are:

- Trade creditors
- Bank overdrafts
- Taxation payable within one year
- Hire purchase payable within one year

The definition of a creditor is a person to whom the business
owes money, such as a supplier.

Net current assets
This is also known as working capital and it is extremely
important. It is the difference between current assets and
current liabilities, and it can be a negative figure if the
liabilities are greater.

It is extremely important, because net current assets are
what is available to finance the day-to-day running of the
business. If net current assets are insufficient for this
purpose the business may have to close or seek some other
form of finance. It is possible for a business to be profitable
but have to close due to a shortage of working capital.

Long-term liabilities
The John Cohen example did not include one, but these are
liabilities which are payable after more than a year. An
example is a fixed-term bank loan. A business may be able
to solve a shortage of working capital by obtaining a long-
term liability in place of a bank overdraft.

Bank overdrafts are invariably legally repayable on demand. This means in theory, and occasionally in practice, that the bank manager can demand repayment at 3 p.m. and if payment has not been received appoint a receiver at 4 p.m. On the other hand, a long-term fixed loan is only repayable when stipulated by the agreement and according to the conditions in the agreement.

Let us consider a 10-year loan of £1 000 000, repayable by 10 equal annual instalments of £100 000. The balance sheet would show £900 000 under long-term liabilities and £100 000 under current liabilities. After a year, and one repayment, the balance sheet would show £800 000 under long-term liabilities and £100 000 under current liabilities. Hire purchase contract balances are split in the same way. The part repayable after a year is shown in long-term liabilities.

A business has an obvious incentive to make as many as possible of its liabilities, long-term liabilities. This eases the pressure on working capital.

Summary

Today we have:

- Understood exactly what a balance sheet is
- Understood how ownership is shown in the accounts
- Seen how balance sheets are laid out and looked at an example
- Prepared a balance sheet
- Studied the main balance sheet headings

Tomorrow, we will round off the week by studying the information provided in published accounts.

Answers
p.76

John Cohen
Balance sheet at April 30th 1995

	£	£
Fixed assets		
Leasehold property	100 000	
Plant and machinery	140 000	
Motor vehicles	30 000	
		270 000
Current assets		
Stock	150 000	
Trade debtors	160 000	
Bank	10 000	
	320 000	
Less current liabilities		
Trade creditors	200 000	
Taxation	80 000	
	280 000	
Net current assets		40 000
		310 000
Capital		
Capital reserve	70 000	
Revenue reserve	240 000	
		310 000

Published accounts

You have now seen how accounts are prepared from the
basic bookkeeping records studied earlier in the week.
Companies are obliged by law to publish their accounts and
we conclude by studying the content and layout of these
published accounts. The programme is:

- How to obtain published accounts
- The obligation to publish accounts
- Companies House
- The obligation to have accounts audited
- What is included in a set of accounts?
- The contents

How to obtain published accounts

Your understanding of today's work will be greatly helped
if you obtain a set of published accounts. A good place to
start is with your employer, assuming that you work for a
company. Your understanding will be increased if the

accounts are of a company that you know, and it will be more interesting as well.

Most public companies are willing to make accounts available to an interested person such as yourself. A request should be made to the company secretary or the public relations office. A telephone call is best and then you should provide an A4 size stamped addressed envelope.

You have the right to obtain a copy of the accounts of any company in the land, public or private, large or small. This can be done by applying to Companies House in Cardiff or one of their offices. It can be done personally for a modest fee. For a larger (but reasonable) fee an agent will do it for you.

The obligation to publish accounts

All companies are required by law to produce accounts annually, though, subject to strict limits, the period can be changed. The law also lays down certain rules about what must be shown in the accounts and how the information must be presented. We will look at this today. Very small companies may file abbreviated accounts.

The law also requires certain organisations other than companies to publish accounts. Building societies are one example. Furthermore, some organisations publish accounts voluntarily. Sole traders and partnerships do not have to publish accounts, except to the Inland Revenue.

Our work today is exclusively with the published accounts of companies.

Companies House

All companies must by law file their accounts at Companies House, where they are open for public inspection. Certain other information must also be filed. A private company must file within 10 months of the balance sheet date at the end of the accounting period. A public company must file within seven months.

Unfortunately, some companies file late or even not at all. This is an offence for which the directors can be fined. Due to more vigorous enforcement procedures, the problem is not so bad as it once was, but it is still a problem. Often, it is the crooked or insolvent companies that do not file. Esther Rantzen and others have pointed this out many times.

The address for companies registered in England and Wales is *The Registrar of Companies, Companies House, Cardiff CF4 3UZ*. At the time of writing there were 903 299 live companies on the register. Companies registered in Scotland, Northern Ireland, Jersey etc. are registered in different offices.

The obligation to have accounts audited

Until recently all company accounts had to be audited by a firm of accountants holding one of the approved qualifications. The regulations have now been changed and this now only applies to a company with an annual turnover of more than £350 000.

An audit is not required if the annual turnover is less than £90 000. If turnover is between £90 000 and £350 000 the accounts must be subject to a compilation report. This is not an audit but an accountant stating that the accounts are compiled from the underlying records. A small company may still choose to have an audit, perhaps to satisfy its bank or the Inland Revenue.

What is included in a set of accounts?

The law sets out certain minimum information that must be included and how it must be presented. Companies can, and often do, provide more than this minimum. Take a look at a set of accounts. You will probably find that it is titled *Directors' Report and Financial Statements* and that it includes the following:

- Chairman's report (may be omitted)
- Directors' report
- Auditor's report
- Profit and loss account
- Balance sheet
- Cash flow statement
- Consolidated accounts (if it is a holding company)
- Explanatory notes

Later today we will consider each in turn.

It is a good idea to familiarise yourself with your set of accounts. See if you can find the answers to the following. The most likely place to find them is given underneath.

1 Do the auditors believe that the accounts give a 'true and fair view'?
2 What were the names of the directors?
3 What was the total of fixed assets at the end of this year and the end of last year?
4 What was spent on fixed assets during the year?
5 What was the profit for the year after tax?
6 What was interest payable in the year?
7 Did the company make any political or charitable contributions?
8 What is the amount of creditors falling due within a year?
9 How is this sum made up?

Where to find the answers
1 Auditor's report
2 Directors' report
3 Balance sheet in both cases
4 Notes
5 Profit and loss account
6 Profit and loss account
7 Directors' report
8 Balance sheet
9 Notes

The contents

We will now take the constituent parts of a set of accounts and consider each part individually. The accounts are usually produced in the order in which they are listed here.

Chairman's report
This is not required by law and is not included in the great majority of accounts of small and medium-sized companies. It is usually, but not always, included in the accounts of public companies.

The chairman's report is a public relations exercise and the chairman can include whatever he wants to include. This may be an appreciation of his fellow directors and the staff, a statement of the company's values and ethical standards, and a tribute to the customers. More usefully it may analyse the business position of the company and its opportunities, the state of the market, and the state of the industry.

It is by no means unusual for a chairman to give his views on the failings of the government, the decline in Western civilisations, and the problems caused by the Chancellor's interest rate policy. He may go on to indulge in special pleading for assistance for his industry and company, making it clear, of course, that his motives are unselfish and that he is motivated only by the interests of the consumer. You will probably have your own views on all these matters and may not be too impressed. It is difficult to generalise as chairman's reports differ so much. Some are very useful and others are not.

Directors' report

The law requires the directors to provide certain information. Much of this may be in the directors' report or elsewhere in the accounts.

The directors' report will usually include the following:

- The principal activity of the business
- A very brief listing of the key figures from the profit and loss account. This may be turnover, profit before tax, tax, dividends, and profit after tax
- A note of dividends paid and proposed
- A listing of the names of directors who held office during some or all of the year, and their dates of appointment or resignation if they did not serve for the whole year
- Details of any disclosable ownership of shares in the company by the directors
- A statement that the reappointment of the auditors will be proposed at the forthcoming annual general meeting. If this is not the intention a different statement may be made

The directors' report will be dated and signed by the company secretary on behalf of the directors.

Auditor's report

The public at large widely misunderstands the purpose and limits of an audit report. The man and woman on the Clapham omnibus typically think that the auditor checks everything and certifies that the accounts are correct. With the possible exception of a very small company this is impossible, and it is not what auditors do.

Auditors test-check the bookkeeping records, and they examine the systems and internal controls. They ask intelligent questions and do reasonable checks of debtors, creditors, stock, fixed assets, etc. They check that the accounts have been prepared from the underlying records.

They then express an opinion as to whether the accounts give a true and fair view. They almost invariably say that they do. This is because most accounts are diligently prepared, and also because it is most definitely not in the interests of the directors for the auditors to say that they do not think that the accounts give a true and fair view. They are therefore likely to agree to the necessary changes.

Seriously qualified audit reports are rare; you will probably not see one and should be wary if you do. Technical qualifications are much more common. This may for example be that the accounts do not completely comply with a certain statement of standard accounting practice.

If an audit report is qualified, a reason will be given. For example it may say that certain money is held in foreign bank accounts, and that it has not been possible to certify the balances and that the money may be readily remitted to the UK. You must exercise your judgement as to the significance of the audit qualification.

The accounts will make it clear that they are the responsibility of the directors. The auditors express an opinion.

Profit and loss account
Most people consider, sometimes wrongly, that the profit and loss account is the most important part of the accounts. They will also consider that the figure for profit before tax is the most important figure in the account. You will probably see the profit and loss account laid out in a similar way to the following. Fictitious figures have been inserted.

	Current year £	Previous year £
Turnover	6 000 000	5 800 000
Less cost of sales	3 000 000	2 700 000
	3 000 000	3 100 000
Less overhead expenses	2 000 000	2 300 000
	1 000 000	800 000
Less interest payable	200 000	160 000
Profit on ordinary activities before tax	800 000	640 000
Less tax on profit on ordinary activities	270 000	210 000
Profit for the year	530 000	430 000
Less dividends paid and proposed	400 000	400 000
Retained profit for the year	130 000	30 000

The retained profit for the year is of course transferred to the balance sheet where it is added to the reserves.

The precise layout of the profit and loss account can vary according to the industry, the circumstances, and the wishes of the directors.

The directors may choose to give a lot more detail than this but it is not usual to do so. You will probably see the key figures with further details given in the notes.

Balance sheet
We studied the balance sheet in detail yesterday and it is normal for the balance sheet in published accounts to be set out in the way shown then. As with the profit and loss account, comparative figures are shown. This means the balance sheet at the start of the trading period is covered by the profit and loss account. Also, like the profit and loss account, it is normal for only the key summarised figures to be shown, further information being given in the notes.

The balance sheet must be signed by two directors on behalf of the board and this copy is lodged with Companies House. The copy that you see will not be signed in ink but the printed names of the two directors will appear, together with the date that they signed. The signing of the balance sheet is not a matter that should be treated lightly. Criminal prosecutions are possible if the directors are fraudulent or reckless.

The published balance sheet will certainly incorporate the following features:

- It will be dated
- It will be cross-referenced to notes
- Fixed assets will be separated from current assets
- Net current assets (working capital) will be shown
- The total of capital and reserves will equal net assets
- Long-term liabilities will be separated from current liabilities

Cash flow statement (formerly called source and applications of funds statement)

To a certain extent profit is a matter of opinion. It depends on the directors' views of the value of stocks, bad debts, the worth of the assets, the adequacy of provisions and many other factors. To be sure, accounting rules and high standards reduce the scope for dispute, but a degree of subjectivity is inevitable.

Cash on the other hand is more a matter of fact. It is either present or it is not. The cash flow statement covers the period of the profit and loss account, which is the period between the two balance sheet dates. The financially sophisticated look to it as an indicator of trouble.

The cash flow statement lists the sources of cash such as normal trading activities, the introduction of new share capital, dividends received, etc.

The cash flow statement also lists the way in which cash has been used such as the payment of tax, payment of dividends, purchase of fixed assets, etc. The difference between the inflow items and the outflow items represents the net inflow or outflow of cash during the period. It corresponds with the change in the bank balances.

Consolidated accounts
It is common for companies to be part of a group and some groups can even contain hundreds of companies. It is obviously misleading if every company in a group prepares accounts without reference to the existence of the group. For this reason every company in a group must disclose the fact of the group and the name of the holding company.

The holding company must prepare consolidated accounts in addition to the accounts for just its own activities. The consolidated balance sheet aggregates the assets and liabilities of all the companies to show the overall position. In doing this, it eliminates debts owing from one group company to another.

The consolidated profit and loss account similarly shows the group profit after eliminating the effect of intergroup trading. This can have a dramatic effect on the turnover when group companies trade with each other. The existence of consolidated accounts does not remove the obligation for every company to prepare and file its own accounts.

Explanatory notes

If it was not for the existence of the notes, the accounts would be unmanageably long. The notes give a breakdown of the summarised figures appearing elsewhere in the accounts. The following are among the items likely to appear in the explanatory notes.

- The accounting policies followed in the preparation of the accounts. These might include, for example, the method of depreciating fixed assets and the basis of the valuation of stocks
- Analysis of turnover by geographical area of the world and by product category
- Details of auditor's remuneration (this must be disclosed by law)
- The emoluments (salary plus benefits) of the highest-paid director. The emoluments of all the other directors must be tabulated in £5 000 bands e.g. three directors got £40 000 – £45 000. Individual names need not be disclosed
- Details of the number of staff employed and the total cost
- Details of the taxation charge
- Details of dividends paid and proposed
- A breakdown of fixed assets showing acquisitions, disposals, depreciation and present values
- Details of stocks held
- Capital commitments and contingent liabilities (e.g. a pending legal action)
- A breakdown of debtors and creditors

Summary

Today we have rounded off our introduction to bookkeeping and accounting by examining published accounts in detail. We have looked at:

- Obtaining published accounts
- The obligation to publish accounts
- Companies House
- The obligation to have accounts audited
- What is in a set of accounts
- The contents in detail

At the end of the week, you should now be able to look at a set of accounts and understand just what is contained within them. You should be able to decipher what the different columns of figures mean and have a firm grasp of all the basic terms and definitions used in accounting. It is worth going over again any sections of the book that you did not quite understand at the time, as progress requires a solid base on which to build. Good luck!